EXPLORING CONTINENTS

AUSTRALIA

Jane Bingham

Heinemann
LIBRARY

www.heinemann.co.uk/library
Visit our website to find out more information about Heinemann Library books.

To order:
 Phone 44 (0) 1865 888066
 Send a fax to 44 (0) 1865 314091
 Visit the Heinemann Bookshop at www.heinemann.co.uk/library to browse our catalogue and order online.

First published in Great Britain by Heinemann, Halley Court, Jordan Hill, Oxford, OX2 8EJ, part of Harcourt Education.

Editorial: Louise Galpine and Harriet Milles
Design: Richard Parker and Q2A Solutions
Illustrations: Jeff Edwards
Picture Research: Mica Brancic and Beatrice Ray
Production: Camilla Crask

Originated by Chroma
Printed and bound in China by WKT

10 digit ISBN 0 431 09745 3 (hardback)
13 digit ISBN 978 0 431 09745 9 (hardback)

11 10 09 08 07
10 9 8 7 6 5 4 3 2 1

British Library Cataloguing in Publication Data
Bingham, Jane
  Australia. - (Exploring continents)
  1. Australia - Geography - Juvenile literature
  I.Title
  919.4
A full catalogue record for this book is available from the British Library.

Acknowledgements
Alamy pp. **16** (Blickwinkel), **23** (Penny Tweedie); Corbis pp. **13** (L.Clarke), **15** (Martin Harvey), **24** (Franz-Marc Frei); Getty pp. **5** (Stone), **9** (National Geographic), **10** (Aurora), **14** (Photonica), **17** (Taxi), **20**, **22** (Stone), **25** (Taxi); Lonely Planet p. **11** (Paul Dymond); NHPA p. **8** (ANT Photo Library); Superstock pp. **7** (Steve Vidler), **27** (Sergio Pitamitz); Travel Ink p. **18**.

Cover satellite image of Australia reproduced with permission of SPL/Planetary Visions Ltd.

Every effort has been made to contact copyright holders of any material reproduced in this book. Any omissions will be rectified in subsequent printings if notice is given to the publishers.

CONTENTS

Words that appear in the text in bold, **like this**, are explained in the Glossary.

WHAT IS A CONTINENT?

A continent is a vast mass of land that covers part of the Earth's surface. There are seven continents in the world – Africa, Antarctica, Asia, Australia, Europe, North America, and South America. Australia is the world's smallest continent.

Where is Australia?

The continental landmass of Australia lies below the **equator**, in the **southern hemisphere.** This means that it has opposite seasons to the northern hemisphere. Winter in Australia lasts from June to August, and summer lasts from December to February.

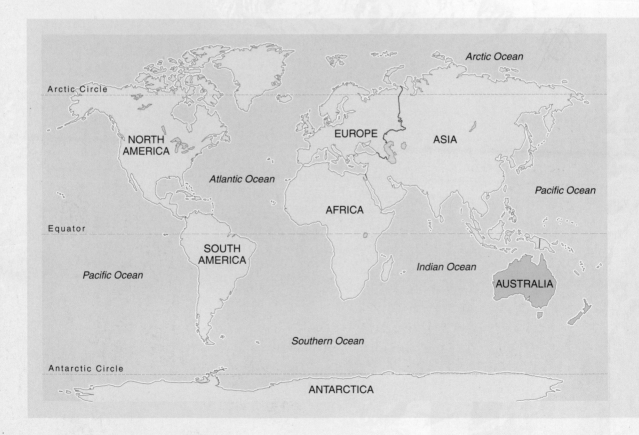

This map shows the seven continents of the world.

Australia is an island with thousands of miles of glorious coastline.

A continent or a country?

Most continents contain several different countries, but Australia is different. It is a continent *and* a country. The country of Australia includes many smaller islands. The largest Australian island is Tasmania. It lies off the coast of South Australia.

When people talk about the Australian continent, they sometimes include New Zealand. In fact, New Zealand is a separate country made up of two islands, which lie to the southwest of Australia. Sometimes, the small islands of the Indian Ocean and the South Pacific Ocean are also grouped with Australia, even though many of them are countries in their own right. Together, all these islands, plus Australia and New Zealand, are known as Oceania. Another name given to all the islands in this region is Australasia.

Did you know?

Australia is almost as large as the continent of Europe, but 30 times more people live in Europe than live in Australia.

WHAT DOES AUSTRALIA LOOK LIKE?

The Australian landscape can be divided into three main regions. Along the eastern coast are rocky **mountain ranges.** In the centre is a vast, low-lying **plain.** In the west of the continent are large areas of high, flat land, known as plateaus.

The central and western areas of Australia are extremely dry and very few people live there. This vast, empty region is often known as the **outback** or the **bush.**

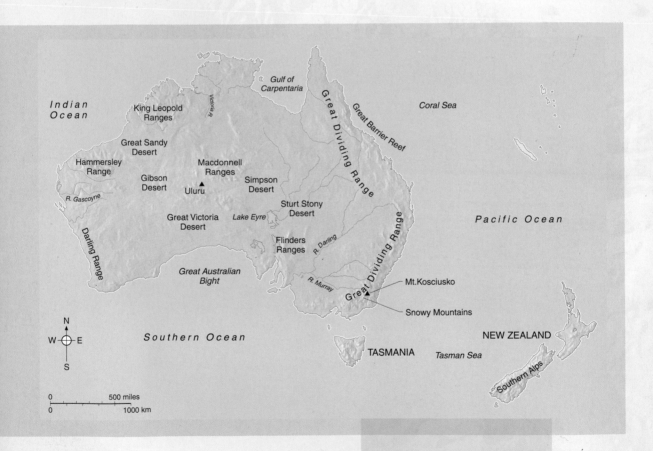

This map shows the different types of landscape in Australia.

Mountains, hills, and rocks

Australia's highest peaks are found in the Great Dividing Range – a long chain of mountains running along the length of the east coast. The Great Dividing Range includes several smaller ranges, such as the Snowy Mountains in South Australia. There are a number of hill ranges scattered over Australia. In the desert, the hills look much higher than they really are, because they rise up suddenly from the flat land.

One of Australia's most spectacular sights is Uluru (also known as Ayers Rock). This giant rock is the world's largest single rock form (or monolith). It is as tall as an 80-floor building.

Uluru rises 335 metres (1,110 ft) above the ground but this is only a third of its total height. The rest of the rock is underground.

Australian deserts

In the centre and west of the continent are many large deserts. Most of these deserts are sandy. However, the Sturt Stony Desert in Central Australia is flat and rocky. Some Australian deserts have massive sand dunes stretching for up to 20 kilometres (12 miles).

This is the Murray-Darling river basin. In the background are the peaks of the Snowy Mountains.

Rivers of Australia

Australia's longest permanently flowing river is the Murray River. Its **source** is the Great Dividing Range and it reaches the sea at the city of Adelaide. Running into the Murray is the Darling River. The land around the meeting place of these two rivers is known as the Murray-Darling basin. The soil in this basin is very good for farming.

Underground water

In central and western Australia, many rivers and streams dry up for several months each year. However, water is still stored deep in the rocks. In some areas, farmers use this underground water. They drill holes into the rock to pump up the salty water.

Australia's lakes

Australia has very few large **freshwater** lakes. However, there are several saltwater lakes south of the Simpson Desert. The largest of these saltwater lakes is Lake Eyre, but it often dries out. During the last century, Lake Eyre filled up with water just three times.

Lake Eyre in South Australia is the continent's largest lake. Most of the time, Lake Eyre is a vast salt marsh, but it fills with water after heavy rains.

The Great Barrier Reef

Running along the northeast coast of Australia is a long shelf of **coral** under the sea. This coral shelf is known as the Great Barrier Reef. Corals are small, water creatures whose skeletons form a colourful, rocky structure. The Great Barrier Reef has built up very slowly over thousands of years.

WHAT IS THE WEATHER LIKE IN AUSTRALIA?

The weather in most of Australia is very hot and dry, and there is a constant danger of fire. However, there are some wetter areas, especially in the continent's northern tip.

Central and western Australia often experience **droughts**, when there is no rain for months. In these dangerously dry conditions, bush fires often break out.

A very dry centre

About one third of Australia is hot, dry desert. In these desert areas, the total rainfall each year is usually less than 250 mm (10 inches). Every day there are long hours of very strong sunshine, and many rivers and streams dry up. At night, temperatures drop dramatically.

The steamy north

The north and northeast corners of Australia are close to the equator. This means that they have a **tropical climate**, with hot, steamy weather and very high rainfall. In the summer temperatures regularly reach 30°C (86°F). During the winter, the weather is still hot, but the air is drier.

From November to March, hot **monsoon** winds from the north bring heavy downpours of rain. Each year, northern Australia has at least 100 mm (40 inches) of rain. During the summer, violent tropical storms, known as typhoons, sometimes strike the coast, causing terrible damage.

During the rainy season, northeast Australia is lashed by sudden downpours of heavy rain.

Cooler places

The south and southeast coast has hot, sunny summers and mild, cool winters. In most parts of this region, winter temperatures never reach freezing point, but the Snowy Mountains are covered with snow each winter. The island of Tasmania to the south has a cooler climate than **mainland** Australia, with rain all year round. Further south, New Zealand has a much colder and wetter climate.

WHAT PLANTS AND ANIMALS LIVE IN AUSTRALIA?

Australia has a wide range of **vegetation**. In the steamy north are tropical **rainforests**. Along the southeast coast are woodlands. The central and western deserts are home to desert plants. To the north and east of the deserts are dry grasslands (sometimes called savannah).

Rainforest plants

The Australian rainforests contain over a thousand **species** of plants that are not found anywhere else in the world. Two unusual rainforest plants are the strangler fig, which gradually chokes trees to death, and the giant stinging tree. The leaves of the giant stinging tree are covered with hairs, which sting any creature that comes into contact with them.

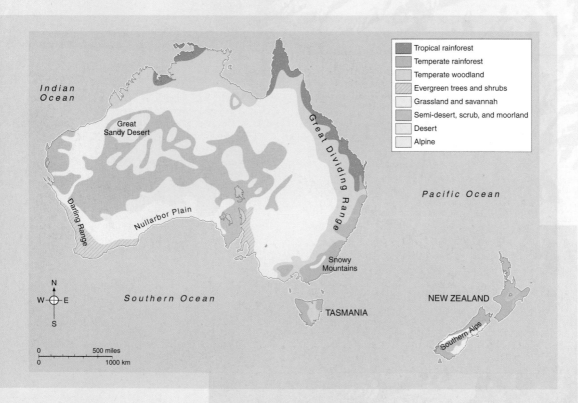

Tropical rainforest
Temperate rainforest
Temperate woodland
Evergreen trees and shrubs
Grassland and savannah
Semi-desert, scrub, and moorland
Desert
Alpine

Indian Ocean

Great Sandy Desert

Great Dividing Range

Pacific Ocean

Darling Range

Nullarbor Plain

Snowy Mountains

N
W—E
S

Southern Ocean

NEW ZEALAND

TASMANIA

Southern Alps

0   500 miles
0   1000 km

This map shows the different types of vegetation in Australia.

Desert plants

In spite of the very harsh climate, some plants survive in the Australian deserts. Clumps of spinifex grass grow on sand dunes, binding the soil together with their powerful roots. The Sturt desert pea is a plant with a scarlet flower that blooms among the rocks in the Sturt Stony Desert. In spite of its name, it does not produce edible peas.

Great gum trees

The most common Australian tree is the eucalyptus or gum tree. Eucalypts were originally rainforest trees but now they are found all over Australia. There are over 500 different types of eucalyptus tree. Their leaves produce strong-smelling oil that is sometimes used in cough sweets.

The leaves of the eucalyptus tree are the main diet of Australia's koala bears.

Did you know?

Eucalyptus trees recover very rapidly from fire. Within a few months of a major forest fire, new shoots start growing from the stumps of burnt-out trees. The shoots sprout from buds that are hidden under the bark of eucalyptus trees.

What makes Australian animals special?

Australia has some very unusual animals. This is because, millions of years ago, the island continent of Australia broke away from a much larger area of land. Then, very gradually, the animals of Australia developed in a different way to those in the rest of the world.

Unusual animals

Many Australian animals are **marsupials**. This means that they carry their young in a pouch. Kangaroos, wallabies, koalas, and wombats are all marsupials. As soon as they are born, marsupial babies crawl up into their mother's pouch. Then they stay in the pouch, feeding on their mother's milk, until they are large enough to survive on their own.

Kangaroos have incredibly powerful legs. They can cover 12 metres (39 ft) of ground in a single bound.

Another of Australia's remarkable animals is the duck-billed platypus. Like all other **mammals**, it has fur and feeds its young with milk. However, instead of giving birth to live babies, the platypus lays eggs like a **reptile**. It is the only survivor of an ancient species of creature that lived 110 million years ago.

Late arrivals

In the 1780s, people from Europe began to settle in Australia. They brought many animals with them – horses, sheep, cows, and pigs, as well as rabbits, cats, and dogs. All these creatures have **adapted** to life in Australia, even though it was not their original home. However, some of these new animals, such as rabbits, have caused problems for Australia's **native** creatures, because they hunt and eat their food.

By the 1980s, rabbits from Europe had almost driven out the native Australian bilby – a marsupial that looks like a small rabbit. Now the number of bilbies is rising again, thanks to a determined **campaign** to save the bilby.

Birds of Australia

Australia has some astonishing birds. The emu is a giant flightless bird that gallops around on long, powerful legs. The kookaburra has a loud, mocking call that sounds like a human laugh, and the rainbow lorikeet is coloured a brilliant green, scarlet, yellow, and blue.

The male lyrebird has very long, curling tail feathers. It is also an expert **mimic**. Lyrebirds have been known to copy the sound of a chainsaw, a barking dog, a car engine revving up, and mobile phones!

The kiwi is only found in New Zealand. Kiwis cannot fly and they have two nostrils on the end of their beak. Today, kiwis are nearly **extinct.**

Insects and spiders

The tropical rainforests of the northeast are swarming with colourful butterflies and beetles. In the Australian deserts, armies of termites (a type of ant) build massive towers from sand and mud. Meanwhile, on the east coast, the deadly funnel-web spider can catch you unawares. Its bite can cause serious illness or even death.

The kookaburra is a member of the kingfisher family. It feeds on snakes and lizards, and is only found in Australia.

Did you know?

Seventeen of the world's most poisonous snakes can be found in Australia. The inland taipan, which lives in the deserts of central Australia, produces one of the most deadly poisons of any snake in the world.

Splendid sea creatures

The warm waters around the Australian coast are home to a fantastic range of creatures, including many species of whales, dolphins, and sharks. The Great Barrier Reef in northeast Australia contains the world's largest collection of coral reefs, with 400 types of coral, 1,500 species of fish, and 4,000 types of shellfish. Also living in the reef are two sea creatures that are in danger of becoming extinct. They are the dugong, or sea cow, and the large green turtle.

Millions of tiny fish swim among the brilliantly coloured corals of the Great Barrier Reef.

WHAT ARE AUSTRALIA'S NATURAL RESOURCES?

Crops, sheep, and cattle

Almost two-thirds of Australia's land is used for farming. In the tropical northwest, sugar cane is the main crop, but mangoes, bananas, and pineapples are also grown. In the eastern highlands, farmers grow wheat, barley, apples, and pears. In southeast Australia, the weather is good for growing grapes and peaches.

In the dry outback, very few crops can grow, but there are vast ranches for sheep and cattle. Sheep are kept mainly for their wool. Teams of expert **shearers** travel from farm to farm, to shear the sheep's wool.

Cattle in the outback are kept mainly for their meat. In the southeast, where the grass grows better, farmers keep dairy cattle. Dairy farmers produce milk, cheese, and yoghurt.

In Australia, there are eight sheep for every one person! Shearing all those sheep is hard work! Experienced shearers can shear around 200 sheep a day.

Mining in Australia

The rocks in Australia's deserts contain gold, uranium, and iron. The continent has the world's biggest diamond mine. Australia also supplies many of the world's opals (a milky-coloured precious stone). Australia is also rich in coal, oil, and natural gas. All these sources of energy are used to provide power for the continent's homes and factories.

The fishing industry

Australian fishing boats catch huge quantities of tuna, marlin, and other smaller fish. They also catch a range of shellfish, including prawns, lobsters, and oysters. Some Australian fish and shellfish are exported to Japan.

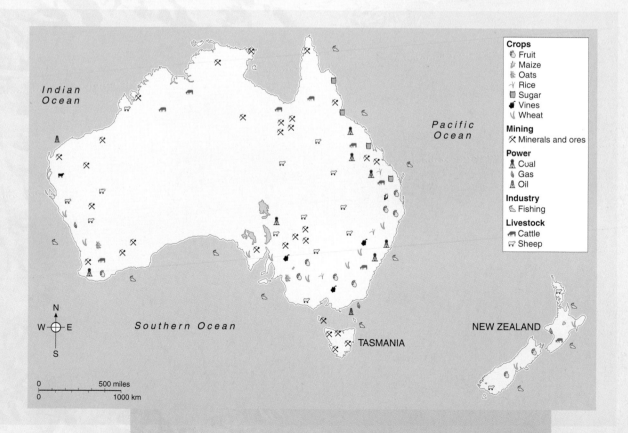

This map shows where Australia's main natural resources can be found.

Manufacturing and other industries

Australia is one of the world's largest producers of processed foods (foods that are packaged or canned in factories). These foods include meat and dairy products, canned fruit, and animal feed. Australia's factories also produce steel machinery, motorcars, plastics, and chemicals.

Making wine

Over the last 20 years, the Australian wine industry has become very successful. South Australia now has over 3,000 **wineries**, and Australian wines are exported all over the world.

The tourist industry

Australia is a popular holiday destination and many Australians work in the tourist industry. Some people work in hotels and restaurants, while others provide sporting and adventure holidays for tourists.

Many young people work as lifeguards on Australia's beaches. They make sure that swimmers and surfers stay safe.

WHAT COUNTRIES AND CITIES ARE IN AUSTRALIA?

The huge country of Australia is divided into six **states** and two **territories**. Each of these areas has its own **government**, but there is also a national government, based in Canberra, Australia's **capital city**. This way of running a country, with a number of states controlled by a national government, is called a federal system.

States and territories

The largest Australian state is Western Australia. The smallest state is the island state of Tasmania. The Australian Capital Territory (usually called A.C.T.) is a thousand times smaller than Western Australia.

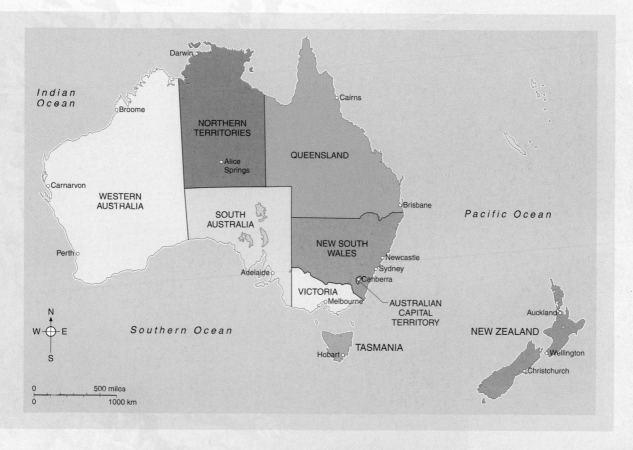

This map shows Australia's states and territories.
It also shows Australia's main cities and towns.

Australia's central government

Australia's central government is similar to the government of Britain. It has a **prime minister** who leads the government and makes important decisions about the country. It also has a **parliament** with members from all over Australia.

Australian cities

Australia's capital city, Canberra, was chosen in 1908. It is home to the national parliament and the national law courts. Each Australian state or territory has its own capital city. Sydney is the capital of New South Wales and Australia's biggest city. It is the continent's most important shipping port, and its main centre for industry and business. One in every five Australians lives in Sydney.

The Australian parliament meets at the Parliament Building in Canberra. This impressive building was opened in 1988.

Did you know?

Everyone in Australia has to vote in a general election. People can be fined if they do not vote.

WHO LIVES IN AUSTRALIA?

Australians come from a wide range of backgrounds. The continent's oldest people are the **Aboriginal Australians**. They have lived in Australia for over 40,000 years. In the 1780s, settlers from Europe began to arrive in the continent.

An Aboriginal Australian artist at work. Aboriginal art often features scenes from the Dreamtime (see box).

The Aboriginal people

For thousands of years, the Aboriginal people lived in small groups all over Australia. They roamed from place to place, and survived by hunting and gathering food. Today, many Aboriginal Australians have moved to Australia's towns and cities. However, some Aboriginals still live in **settlements** in the outback. These settlements are mainly found in northern and central Australia.

Did you know?

The Aboriginal people believe that the Australian landscape was created thousands of years ago in a time called the Dreamtime. According to their beliefs, powerful spirits made journeys across the land creating hills, rocks, and rivers, and also plants, animals, and humans. Aboriginal artists paint pictures of the Dreamtime.

Settlers from abroad

In 1788, people from Britain set up the first **colonies** in Australia. Many British prisoners were sent from Britain to work in the colonies, building houses and roads. British and Irish farmers also settled in Australia. In the 1850s, gold was discovered. Goldmines were built, and many people arrived from China to work in the mines. Since the 1940s, more than five million people from Europe and Asia have moved to Australia.

Town life

More than 80 percent of Australians live in towns and cities. Australian cities are very spread out, with large **suburbs** surrounding the city centre.

In Melbourne, Victoria, people enjoy the sunshine in outdoor cafés.

Many Australian farms are so huge that people have to drive for miles to see their neighbours.

Country life

People in the country are mainly farmers or miners. In very remote areas, there is a 'flying doctor' service. If people become seriously ill, a doctor arrives by plane to take them to the

Did you know?

Australia has a 'School of the Air' for children who live in remote country areas. The school broadcasts lessons on radio and TV. Some country children also use phone and e-mail to contact their teachers.

WHAT FAMOUS PLACES ARE IN AUSTRALIA?

Natural wonders

On Australia's east coast is the Great Barrier Reef, with its colourful corals and amazing sea creatures (see pages 9 and 17). In the heart of the continent is the massive rock known as Uluru (see page 7). In the northwest, Kakadu National Park is well known for its birds and animals, and its ancient Aboriginal rock paintings.

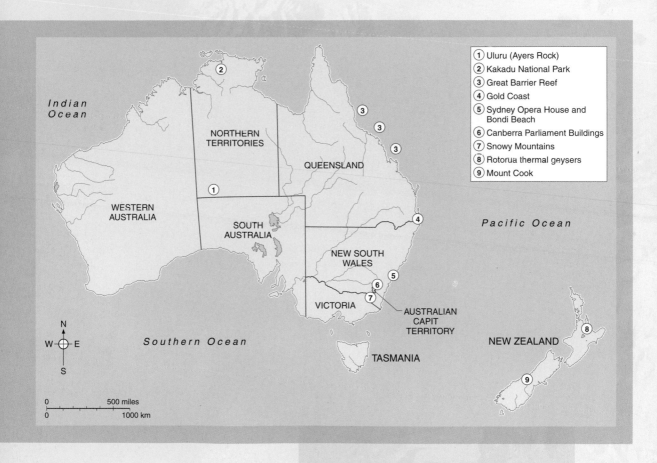

① Uluru (Ayers Rock)
② Kakadu National Park
③ Great Barrier Reef
④ Gold Coast
⑤ Sydney Opera House and Bondi Beach
⑥ Canberra Parliament Buildings
⑦ Snowy Mountains
⑧ Rotorua thermal geysers
⑨ Mount Cook

This map shows where some of Australia's famous places are found.

Beautiful beaches

Australia is world famous for its beaches. Sydney's Bondi Beach is always filled with surfers and tourists. The Gold Coast in eastern Australia has miles of sandy beaches with excellent waves for surfing.

Lively cities

Sydney, Melbourne, Brisbane, and Perth are all thriving ports. Each of these cities has a lively business centre and plenty of tourist attractions.

The Sydney Opera House is one of the world's best known buildings. It is an unforgettable sight, perched beside the sparkling water of Sydney harbour.

CONTINENTS COMPARISON CHART

Continent	Area	Population	
AFRICA	30,365,000 square kilometres (11,720,000 square miles)	906 million	
ANTARCTICA	14,200,000 square kilometres (5,500,000 square miles)	officially none, but about 4,000 people live on the research stations during the summer and over 3,000 people visit as tourists each year. People have lived there for as long as three and a half years at a time.	
ASIA	44,614,000 square kilometres (17,226,200 square miles)	almost 4,000 million	
AUSTRALIA	7,713,364 square kilometres (2,966,136 square miles)	approximately 20,090,400 (2005 estimate)	
EUROPE	10,400,000 square kilometres (4,000,000 square miles)	approximately 727 million (2005 estimate)	
NORTH AMERICA	24,230,000 square kilometres (9,355,000 square miles)	approximately 509,915,000 (2005 estimate)	
SOUTH AMERICA	17,814,000 square kilometres (6,878,000 square miles)	380 million	

Number of Countries	Highest Point	Longest River
54 (includes Western Sahara)	Mount Kilimanjaro, Tanzania — 5,895 metres (19,340 feet)	Nile River — 6,695 kilometres (4,160 miles)
none, but over 23 countries have research stations in Antarctica	Vinson Massif — 4,897 metres (16,067 feet)	River Onyx — 12 kilometres (7.5 miles) **Biggest Ice Shelf** Ross Ice Shelf in western Antarctica — 965 kilometres (600 miles) long.
50	Mount Everest, Tibet and Nepal — 8,850 metres (29,035 feet)	Yangtze River, China — 6,300 kilometres (3,914 miles)
1	Mount Kosciusko — 2,229 metres (7,313 feet)	Murray River — 2,520 kilometres (1,566 miles)
47	Mount Elbrus, Russia — 5,642 metres (18,510 feet)	River Volga — 3,685 kilometres (2,290 miles)
23	Mount McKinley (Denali) in Alaska — 6,194 metres (20,320 feet)	Mississippi/Missouri River System — 6,270 kilometres (3,895 miles)
12	Aconcagua, Argentina — 6,959 metres (22,834 feet)	Amazon River — 6,400 kilometres (4,000 miles)

GLOSSARY

Aboriginal Australians first people to live in Australia

adapt to change behaviour in order to fit into new surroundings

bush dry, unfarmed land in the centre of Australia

campaign series of actions that are meant to make something happen

capital city city where a country's government is based

climate kind of weather that an area has

colony area where people from another country have settled, which is controlled by that other country

coral small water creatures whose skeletons remain after they have died, forming a colourful, rocky structure

drought long period of very dry weather

equator imaginary line running around the middle of the Earth

export sending goods abroad to be sold

extinct no longer existing anywhere on Earth

freshwater water that does not contain salt

general election time when the people in a country vote to choose their next government

government group of people who rule or govern a state or country

mainland main area of a country, rather than the islands around it

mammal animal that feeds its young on its own milk

marsupial kind of mammal whose females carry their young in a pouch

mimic bird, animal, or person who is very good at copying the behaviour of others

monsoon season of very heavy rain and strong winds

mountain range lots of mountains in a row

native belonging to a place

outback dry, unfarmed land in the centre of Australia

parliament group of people who make the laws of a country

plain large, level area of land

prime minister leader of the government in some countries

rainforest thick forest where lots of rain falls

reptile animal with a scaly skin that lays eggs. Lizards, snakes, and turtles are all reptiles.

settlement place where people settle down and make their homes

shearer someone who cuts the wool off sheep

single-storey with ground floor only

source place where a river starts

southern hemisphere all the land that lies below the equator, in the southern half of the globe

species type of animal or plant

state area in a country that makes its own laws

suburb area of housing on the edge of a city or town

territory area in Australia similar to a state, but with a slightly different system of government

tropical hot, rainy, and steamy

vegetation plants, bushes, and trees

winery farm where wine is produced

FURTHER INFORMATION

Books

Aboriginal Art and Culture, Jane Bingham (Raintree, 2005)

Continents: Australia and Oceania, Leila Merrell Foster (Heinemann Library, 2002)

Countries of the World: Australia, Robert Prosser (Evans Brothers, 2004)

Country File: Australia, Dana M. Rau (Franklin Watts, 2002)

Useful websites

- The highly illustrated website of *Australian Geographic Magazine*:
  http://editorial.australiangeographic.com.au/
- A well-organized guide to Australia with links to related websites:
  http://www.csu.edu.au/australia/
- A site on Aboriginal culture and art:
  http://www.aboriginalaustralia.com/aboriginal.htm

Disclaimer

All the internet addresses (URLs) given in this book were valid at the time of going to press. However, due to the dynamic nature of the internet, some addresses may have changed, or sites may have ceased to exist since publication. While the author and publishers regret any inconvenience this may cause readers, no responsibility for such changes can be accepted by either the author(s) or the publishers.

INDEX

Titles in the Exploring Continents series include:

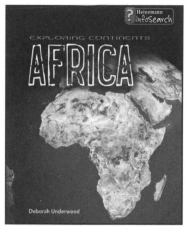

Deborah Underwood

Hardback   0 431 09742 9

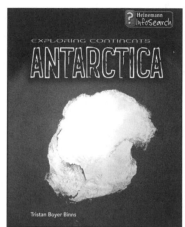

Tristan Boyer Binns

Hardback   0 431 09743 7

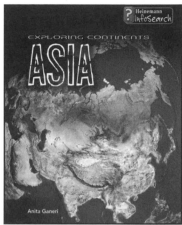

Anita Ganeri

Hardback   0 431 09744 5

Jane Bingham

Hardback   0 431 09745 3

Jane Bingham

Hardback   0 431 09746 1

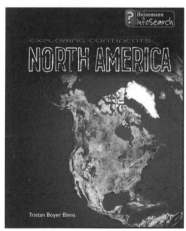

Tristan Boyer Binns

Hardback   0 431 09747 X

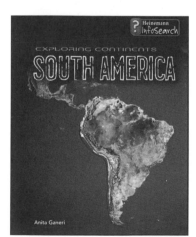

Anita Ganeri

Hardback   0 431 09748 8

Find out about other titles from Heinemann Library on our website www.heinemann.co.uk/library